William M
Designing an
Earthly Paradise

3   Introduction

8   Textiles
    Cory Korkow

24 The Kelmscott Press
    Victoria Hepburn

40 Further Readings

Installation view of the bed
hangings embroidered by
May Morris, her friends,
and students at the
Birmingham School of Art

Introduction

"Time was when everybody that made anything made a work of art besides a useful piece of goods, *and it gave them pleasure to make it.* Whatever I doubt, I have no doubt of that."[1]
—William Morris

Astonishingly energetic, William Morris was a poet, craftsman, designer, novelist, businessman, preservationist, painter, and social activist. A doctor attributed his cause of death in 1896 at age 62 to "simply being William Morris, and having done more work than most ten men."[2] Like any prolific and complex person, Morris can be approached from numerous perspectives. This exhibition focuses on his artistic output—namely, two-dimensional designs for textiles and the printed page. Textile design fascinated Morris particularly during the 1860s and 1870s, while his aspirations for book design came to fruition with the Kelmscott Press in the 1890s. The Cleveland Museum of Art is fortunate to have several of Morris's most iconic textiles in its collection and, in its Ingalls Library, a complete run of the 53 books printed by Kelmscott Press.

At the turn of the 19th century, Cleveland was one of the largest and most prosperous cities in the nation, and the Arts and Crafts movement that had begun in England could be felt in the way fashionable Clevelanders designed and furnished their homes. Morris & Co. products such as wallpaper and textiles were available to American consumers through the firm's authorized

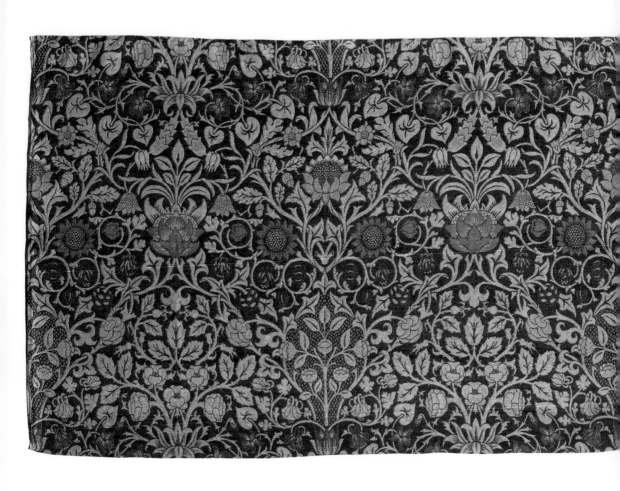

agent in New York, as well as at department stores in Boston as early as 1873 and at Chicago's Marshall Field & Company by the mid-1880s. Chicago businessman John Glessner decorated his Arts and Crafts home—now a museum—with Morris fabrics, wallpapers, ceramics, and custom-made carpets.[3] The fact that stylish Clevelanders were also attracted to William Morris's designs is borne out in several bequests to the museum. The block-printed textiles *Peony, Marigold, Honeysuckle, Snakeshead, Strawberry Thief,* and *Kennet* were donated in 1937 by Mrs. Henry Chisholm (née Louise Brigham), whose late husband was the grandson of Henry Chisholm—referred to as the "father of the Cleveland steel trade." Between 1937 and 1953, Mrs. Philip White (née Gladys McNairy) gifted *Tulip* and two jacquard-woven textiles, *Peacock and Dragon* and *Violet and Columbine.* Gladys was the granddaughter of George Willis Pack, who had purchased *Violet and Columbine* in the mid-1880s most likely to use as curtains in his mansion on Cleveland's Euclid Avenue (then known as Millionaires' Row) (fig. 1).[4] Gladys was involved in the Textile Arts Club at the museum and exhibited her own embroidery at the annual May Show. While the textiles were acquired from wealthy families with established relationships to the museum, William H. and Julia Morgan Marlatt's gift of Kelmscott Press books in 1939 came as a surprise, discussed here in Victoria Hepburn's essay.

The installation of *William Morris: Designing an Earthly Paradise* reflects the character of many Victorian rooms that incorporated Morris & Co. products (fig. 2). Richly varied designs on fabric, wallpaper, and carpets produced a vividly lush effect that may seem like a cacophony of patterns to today's minimalist design sensibilities. The gallery walls are papered with a modern reproduction of *Fruit*, one of Morris's earliest wallpaper

Fig. 2. Installation view
of modern reproductions
of Morris & Co.'s *Fruit*
wallpaper and *Bullerswood*
carpet

designs, which was inspired by the garden at the Morris family's country estate, Red House. This pattern has been in continuous production since its design in 1862. The Victoria and Albert Museum assisted with reproducing a full-scale replica on vinyl of its carpet *Bullerswood*. Co-designed by John Henry Dearle, who later served as art director of Morris & Co., it was the largest hand-knotted Hammersmith carpet (so called for the district where they were originally produced) that the firm created.[5] We invite you to immerse yourself in the 19th-century world of William Morris, brought into the 21st century.

Cory Korkow
Associate Curator of European Art

1. John W. Mackail, *The Life of William Morris*, vol. 2 (London: Longmans, Green, 1899), 20.

2. Mackail, 2:336.

3. Bruce Smith, *The Beautiful Necessity: Decorating with Arts & Crafts*, 2nd ed. (Layton, UT: Gibbs Smith, 2009), 17.

4. Dan Ruminski and Alan Dutka, *Cleveland in the Gilded Age: A Stroll Down Millionaires' Row* (Charleston, SC: History Press, 2012). The Pack (McNairy) home was demolished in 1953.

5. Linda Parry, *William Morris Textiles* (London: V&A Publishing, 2013), 117–21.

Textiles

"If a chap can't compose an epic poem while he's weaving
tapestry, he had better shut up, he'll never do any good at all."[1]
—William Morris

An exacting designer and businessman, Morris possessed a
meticulousness that caused both anxiety and admiration among
his collaborators. He also insisted on fair labor conditions for his
workers, which set him apart from many Victorian manufacturers
for whom industrialism meant imposing grueling hours for low
wages in dangerous factories. The decorative arts firm Morris,
Marshall, Faulkner & Co.—founded in 1862 and reconstituted as
Morris & Co. after 1875—designed and sold household furnishings
that were sought after for their elegant and colorful patterns and
high-quality materials (fig. 3). Much of the integrity and beauty of
Morris's designs can be attributed to his conviction that one should
intimately know a process, both mentally and physically, before
embarking on a design. A self-taught embroiderer, wood engraver,
and weaver, he also resurrected numerous long-forgotten crafts
related to book design and illumination, dyeing, and stained glass.

During an age when rooms were stuffed with mass-produced
objects and teemed with gratuitous ornament, Morris challenged
consumers to embrace harmony and restraint in decoration:
"Have nothing in your houses that you do not know to be useful,
or believe to be beautiful."[2] Throughout his career, however, a ten-
sion existed between his desire to make high-quality handcrafted

goods widely available and the expense of producing them from fine materials. This meant that primarily only the wealthy could afford them. Although Morris was often called upon to supervise the decoration of homes of aristocrats and newly wealthy industrialists, and even the Throne Room of Queen Victoria, the commissions ran contrary to his increasingly social-activist principles. Exasperated by one patron who asked what troubled him, Morris complained, "It's just that I spend my life ministering to the swinish luxury of the rich."[3] A similar paradox shaped Morris's own life. He had a conventional, upper-middle-class background; family shares in Devon copper mines helped support him through an elite education at Oxford University and in early business endeavors. He originally planned to enter the church, but at Oxford he met life-long friend Edward Burne-Jones. Both men succumbed to the lure of medieval literature and history, eventually choosing artistic, creative professions.

g. 3. Interior of Morris Co.'s shop on George reet, London. Featured the company's *Change Address* brochure, 1917. Courtesy of the 'illiam Morris Gallery, ondon

Morris was introduced to church embroidery during his brief apprenticeship to architect George Edmund Street, whose sister co-founded the Ladies Ecclesiastical Embroidery Society, which produced the finest Victorian church embroideries. Lodging with Burne-Jones in the former Bloomsbury studio of Pre-Raphaelite painter Dante Gabriel Rossetti, in 1857 Morris began designing furnishings and even embroidered his adopted motto, "If I can," on a woolen hanging. However, it was Morris's marriage in 1859 to Jane Burden and the subsequent need to furnish Red House— designed by his friend Philip Webb—that sparked the vision for a decorative arts firm. For Morris, the pleasure of making useful and beautiful objects, as with traveling or reading poetry, was a joy that became magnified when shared with others; his ideal productive environment was a community of creators. From his university days through the end of his life, he thrived on the intellectual and visual stimulation of friends and family, a microcosm for the exemplary labor conditions he strove for in his workshops. Morris gathered together his friends Burne-Jones, Rossetti, and Webb, as well as artist Ford Madox Brown, mathematician

Fig. 4. The Burne-Jones and Morris families. Photo: Frederick Hollyer. © National Portrait Gallery, London

Charles Faulkner, and civil engineer Peter Marshall, and together they founded the most influential design firm of the Arts and Crafts movement (fig. 4). Many in his circle designed and created the firm's products, and although their individual voices have grown increasingly silent over time, they were once actively featured, and several are singled out here.

Textiles—including embroidery, printed cotton, woven fabrics, tapestries, and carpets—were among the most profitable of the company's merchandise. In the spring of 1876 when he was in the midst of one of his most productive periods of textile design, an energetic Morris wrote to his friend Aglaia Coronio, "I am drawing patterns so fast that last night I dreamed I had to draw a sausage; somehow I had to eat it first, which made me anxious about my digestion: however I have just done quite a pretty pattern for printed work."[4] While we do not know to which work this anecdote refers, it was written the year he designed *Honeysuckle*, an archetypal pattern that shows his love of large mirror motifs (fig. 5). This one extends almost the

Fig. 5. *Honeysuckle*, design registered 1876. William Morris. Bleached linen: plain weave, block printed. The Cleveland Museum of Art, Gift of Mrs. Henry Chisholm, 1937.697

Fig. 6. *Peony*, design registered 1877. Kate Faulkner (British, 1841–1898). Cotton: plain weave, block printed. The Cleveland Museum of Art, Gift of Mrs. Henry Chisholm, 1937.700

entire 35-inch-plus width of the loom. Morris believed that large patterns were more restful to the eye than small ones, even when used to decorate modestly sized rooms.

The small, almost square repeat of *Peony* noticeably differs from *Honeysuckle* (fig. 6). The likely designer was Kate Faulkner, the sister of Morris's early business partner. She also designed embroidery, wallpaper, painted tiles and pottery, and plaster decoration for the firm. Morris had a progressive attitude toward women as co-laborers, and promoted the work of designers such as Kate, whose inventive patterns challenged the monotony of much of the needlework and domestic crafts that occupied middle-class women in Victorian Britain. In its shop, the firm also sold the magnificent and costly embroideries of Morris's friend and renowned embroiderer Catherine Holiday, keeping only 10 percent of the sale price.[5]

Strongly influenced by English art critic John Ruskin's evocation of the medieval stone carver—whose pride in his work is reflected in the dignity of its form[6]—Morris believed that when not linked to mass production, specialized labor permitted workers to express their particular skills such as designing, weaving, or carving. For example, the firm's textiles were printed with hand-carved woodblocks rather than by the dominant roller method. Woodblocks could be cut with more dynamic patterns and finessed by the printer, while the round roller mechanically churned out lengths of static ornament (fig. 7).

Fig. 7. Woodblock used for printing *Tulip*, c. late 800s. Courtesy of the William Morris Gallery, London

Morris was a gifted pattern maker and looked to both nature
and history as a model. Unlike German and Japanese textile designers, or his English competitors, he was inspired not by exotic
greenhouse flowers but by the simple blooms found in an English
garden. Tulips appear in many of Morris's designs, underscoring
the importance of commonly cultivated garden flowers for his
patterns (fig. 8). The humble marigold, honeysuckle, tulip, and
sunflower often joined tangled ivy or sprigs of willow in patterns
of great clarity and charm. "Rational growth" was the underlying
principle of Morris's patterns, which were revolutionary in their
depiction of blossoms and vines spreading with ordered freedom,

generating a sense of movement that set them apart from the rigid, formal patterns dominating the market. Although it was among his first designs for printing on fabric, *Marigold* was originally intended for use on wallpaper (fig. 9). It was one of only a few patterns that the firm produced as both textile and wallpaper, since Morris's sensitivity to the flatness of a wallpaper, as opposed to a textile's ability to fold and drape, meant that he regarded their design needs as different.

Morris & Co.'s earliest textiles from the 1860s were intended to emulate the medieval tapestries Morris and his friends admired and imagined to have hung on stone-cold walls. Registered in

Fig. 10. *Peacock and Dragon*, design registered 1878. William Morris. Wool: Jacquard loom–woven; weft-faced, twill weave. The Cleveland Museum of Art, Gift of Mrs. Philip White, 1953.330

1878, *Peacock and Dragon* is the closest Morris came to achieving this ideal by incorporating a bold design and soothing colors with warm, thick wool (fig. 10). In the same year he created this textile, Morris had visited Vincent Robinson's London shop where he saw a re-created room from Damascus, "all vermillion and gold and ultramarine, very beautiful, and is just like going into the Arabian nights."[7] The display partly inspired the exotic motifs in *Peacock and Dragon*, one of the most popular among Morris's customers; it was available in five colorways. When Morris designed *Snakeshead* in 1877, Indian silks were in style and widely imported from British India (fig. 11). This design stands out for its diminutive motifs and strong colors of red and black, which were fashionable only for a short time before paler hues regained favor with clients. While its color scheme suggested distant lands,

the pattern showcases one of Morris's favorite flowers: the fritillary, a wildflower that he remembered growing in the meadows near Oxford.

During the second half of the 19th century, garish and fugitive chemical dyes became standard in industrialized England. One of Morris's more costly innovations was returning to organic dyes, which were expensive and scarce, and required skilled dyers willing to revive old processing methods. However, organic dyes were less likely to fade in the light or during washing, and they were capable of producing tonal effects that were both richer and subtler. Among the natural dyes used in Morris & Co. textiles are cochineal, derived from the so-called insect that has been used for centuries to create a red dye, and weld or dyer's rocket, a flowering weed that produces a vibrant yellow tone (fig. 12).

Fig. 12. (*Left to right*) Examples of the natural dyes weld, cochineal, and indigo

The firm also used indigo as the foundational color for many textiles. Beginning in 1881, Morris had textiles dyed, printed, and woven at Merton Abbey, a village on the River Wandle in Surrey. The enterprise was described as a "colossal kindergarten for adults";[8] Morris's own dyeing experiments often left him with hands stained blue for days.

Morris perfected the indigo-discharge process with *Strawberry Thief*, which required the entire cloth to be dyed blue before being bleached and block printed, in this case with more colors than any other Morris textile (fig. 13). Perhaps the most enduringly popular of his textiles, *Strawberry Thief* celebrates the thrushes in the garden at Kelmscott Manor, the 16th-century country home where the Morris family decamped from London after 1871. Morris's daughter May later remarked, "You can picture my Father going

out in the early morning and watching the rascally thrushes at work on the fruit-beds and telling the gardener who growls, 'I'd like to wring their necks!' that no bird in the garden must be touched."[9]

An avid student of history and a voracious collector, Morris said that he used the South Kensington Museum (now the Victoria and Albert Museum) more than anyone alive. In fact, he became one of the most knowledgeable textile historians of the period. His love of nature, filtered through the lens of history, resulted in unconventional patterns that are simultaneously familiar and fresh. With their strong diagonal orientation, his later textiles such as *Kennet* show a debt to the Italian cut velvet that he had studied (figs. 14, 15). *Kennet*, named after a river in the south of England that flows into the Thames, is an example of a Morris pattern that could be purchased in a variety of colors and fabrics, including cotton, velveteen, silk, and Madras muslin. This created endless possibilities for consumers to customize products based on their needs and taste. His exquisitely detailed and colorful design drawing in the Birmingham Museum of Art conveys the care with which he conceived the relationship of form and color (fig. 16).

Morris's creativity was fueled by his family's support of and involvement in his work, a tradition and practice then continued by his daughter May. The American novelist Henry James, describing a visit to the Morrises in 1869, mentioned that May, then seven years old, assisted her family in creating a "tapestry."[10] May became an influential designer and accomplished needlewoman. In 1885, at age 23, she took over the highly successful embroidery branch of Morris & Co., producing designs and supervising production. From the late 1870s, her father felt increasingly strained with overseeing the embroiderers, and with May at the helm he was able to focus on other branches of production. May was also active as an instructor at a number of embroidery schools. In 1907 she co-founded the Women's Guild of Arts because the Art Workers Guild—established in 1884 with the goal of uniting fine and applied arts—did not admit women.

Fig. 14. *Silk Fragment*, 1350–99. Italy. Silk and gold thread: lampas weave. The Cleveland Museum of Art, Dudley P. Allen Fund, 1940.1193

20

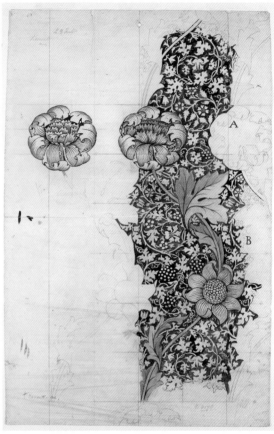

Fig. 15. *Kennet*, design
registered 1883. William
Morris. Indigo-discharged
cotton: plain weave, block
printed. The Cleveland
Museum of Art, Gift of
Mrs. Henry Chisholm,
1937.698

Fig. 16. *Printed Fabric
Design—Kennet*, 1883.
William Morris. Pencil,
watercolor on paper
touched with white; 101.1
x 66.7 cm. Birmingham
Museums, Purchased

from Morris & Co.
through Friends of
Birmingham Museums
and Art Gallery, 1940,
1941P404. Photo ©
Birmingham Museums
Trust

May adopted many of her father's design principles, but her particular contribution as a designer of embroidery was as a bold colorist. While her father was notoriously clumsy at drawing and incorporating birds and other creatures into his designs, May embraced the union between flora and fauna. This is visible in the birds and charming squirrels on the curtains that formed part of a suite of bed hangings embroidered by May, her friends, and students at the Birmingham School of Art (fig. 17). Subtle variations in the treatment of the same bird by a different hand, from one curtain to the other, show how an individual embroiderer's style

Fig. 17. *Bed hangings: two curtains and one valance,* 1916. May Morris (British, 1862–1938), designer. Embroidered by May Morris, Mary J. Newill, Dora Webb, G. Cattell, A. B. Simpson, Isobel Catterson-Smith, Mrs. Moore, Nan Hornby, M. Dalton, and Wilhelmina Edelstein. Wool on linen; 194.9 x 68.6 cm. Cranbrook Art Museum, Gift of George Gough Booth and Ellen Scripps Booth, 1955, CAM 1955.402

and skill are discernible in a group endeavor. The brightly colored bed hangings display the influence of traditional crewelwork, a manner of embroidering wool on linen that was popular in 17th-century Britain. They were first shown as part of a "lady's bedroom" at the Arts and Crafts Exhibition Society's 1916 exhibition in London. Priced at £170, the bedstead and hangings would have been prohibitively expensive for middle- or lower-class women. In 1920 they appeared in the *Exhibition of British Arts & Crafts* in Detroit, where they were purchased by George Booth, the founder of Cranbrook Art Academy. He used them in his home until they were given to the Cranbrook Art Museum in 1955.

Morris & Co. disbanded in 1940, almost five decades after William Morris's death. John Henry Dearle, a talented designer apprenticed to Morris at an early age, ran the firm in its later years, and it continued to produce classic designs by William and May Morris, Edward Burne-Jones, and Kate Faulkner, among others. Many of these designs are still available to consumers in a bewildering array of colors, materials, and forms inconceivable even to the visionary Morris.

Cory Korkow is the museum's associate curator of European art.

1. Mackail, 1:186.

2. Mackail, 2:63–64.

3. Quoted in William Richard Lethaby, *Philip Webb and His Work* (London: Raven Oak, 1979), 94.

4. William Morris, *The Collected Works of William Morris: With Introductions by His Daughter May Morris* (Cambridge: Cambridge University Press, 2012), vii.

5. Parry, 31.

6. John Ruskin, *The Stones of Venice*, vol. 2, *The Sea-Stories* (London: Smith, Elder, 1853).

7. William Morris, letter to May Morris, March 21, 1878.

8. Pamela Todd, *William Morris and the Arts and Crafts Home* (San Francisco: Chronicle Books, 2005), 108.

9. May Morris, ed., *William Morris: Artist, Writer, Socialist*, vol. 1 (Oxford: Basil Blackwell, 1936), 45.

10. Percy Lubbock, ed., *The Letters of Henry James*, vol. 1 (New York: Charles Scribner's Sons, 1920), 17.

VICTORIA HEPBURN

The Kelmscott Press

"The picture-book . . . must remain one of the very worthiest things towards the production of which reasonable men should strive."[1]
—William Morris

The lofty conclusion to William Morris's lecture "The Ideal Book," quoted above, reveals the gravity with which he approached his last, great undertaking: the Kelmscott Press, which consumed the final, busy years of his life. Morris established the press in 1890 with the help of master printer Emery Walker, editor F. S. Ellis, and a cadre of accomplished illustrators, engravers, and pressmen. When asked by a reporter why he embarked upon the project, Morris simply stated, "I wanted to print some nice books. Also I wanted to amuse myself."[2] This rather modest answer disguises the true scale of Morris's venture. "Some" books amounted to 53 individual titles, many with editions numbering more than 300. Far from merely "nice," each is an intricate work of art thoughtfully produced to reflect Morris's unwavering belief in the edifying power of good design and solid craftsmanship. Kelmscott, named after the designer's 16th-century country manor in Oxfordshire, became the English-speaking world's best-known private press. Its productions both visually and ideologically influenced book design well into the 20th century, and arguably beyond.

Morris dreamed of starting a printing press after attending a lecture on book illustration and printing given by his friend and neighbor Emery Walker at the first annual exhibition of the Arts and Crafts Exhibition Society in 1888. For his lecture, Walker sourced specimens from Morris's collection of early printed books and writing manuals. He projected enlarged, glowing images of woodcut illustrations and late-medieval types before a wildly enthusiastic crowd, including the writer and aesthete Oscar Wilde. None, however, was more eager than Morris himself.[3]

Long interested in the book arts, Morris had focused his energies mostly on creating single, handmade manuscripts before founding his press. Several of these were exquisitely ornamented and illustrated with the help of his lifelong friend and artistic kindred spirit Edward Burne-Jones; other colleagues from his design firm Morris, Marshall, Faulkner & Co. also contributed. *A Book of Verse*, made for Burne-Jones's wife, Georgiana, delightfully exemplifies this pre-Kelmscott foray into book design (fig. 18). Completed in 1870, the manuscript is filled with Morris's intricate calligraphy. Elaborate, vegetative borders and initials—some drawn by the artist and manager of Morris's firm, George Wardle—burst from the pages. Burne-Jones and the designer Charles Fairfax Murray painted the colorful illustrations. The book is a manifesto on the power of artistic collaboration that is reminiscent of medieval workshop practice.

Fig. 18. *Meeting in Winter*, from *A Book of Verse*, 1870. William Morris. Calligraphy in ink and gilt; paginated in gilt; vellum binding, tooled in gold with floral ornaments. Victoria and Albert Museum, London, MSL/1953/131. © Victoria and Albert Museum, London

Fig. 20. *The Legend of Cupid and Psyche: Psyche, Seeking Death, about to Leap into the Stream,* 1865–68. Workshop of William Morris, after Edward Burne-Jones. Wood engraving; 10.5 x 8.2 cm. The Cleveland Museum of Art, Gift of the Print Club of Cleveland, 1981.90

Fig. 19. *Morris at a table working on a woodblock,* from an album of 60 caricature drawings, c. 1886. Edward Burne-Jones (British, 1833–1898). Graphite; 8 x 9.8 cm. The British Museum, London, 1939,0513.23. © The Trustees of the British Museum

Arguably more famous in the 19th century for his writing than for his design work, Morris had a large stake in the state of Victorian printing. He keenly felt that texts suffered when produced with undue expediency on cheap paper and with little thought given to their illustrations or typography, as was often the case. He understood that the material elements of a book—the experience of touching and turning the page, the visual impact of each page seen as a uniform design—held as much power as the written word. In the mid-1860s, he and Burne-Jones set out to print a sumptuous version of Morris's most famous poem, *The Earthly Paradise,* with more than 200 wood-engraved illustrations. Morris cut many of Burne-Jones's designs himself. A charming caricature by the artist shows Morris carrying out this meticulous task (fig. 19). A print of a completed illustration, *The Legend of Cupid and Psyche: Psyche, Seeking Death, about to Leap into the*

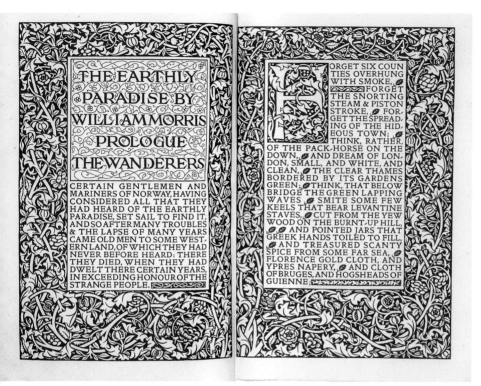

Stream, appears in this exhibition (fig. 20). The ambitious project
was never realized. With no appropriate typeface to reflect the
bold illustrations designed to emulate medieval woodcuts, the
trial pages fell flat; text and image failed to achieve the visual
harmony Morris sought so fervently.[4] Not until the founding of
the Kelmscott Press was *The Earthly Paradise* printed in a manner
worthy of its literary grandeur (fig. 21).

Disenchanted by the unrealized illustrated *Earthly Paradise*
and frustrated by the lack of suitable typefaces, Morris designed
one as his first order of business at the Kelmscott Press.[5] Using
Emery Walker's modern photographic methods as a design aid,

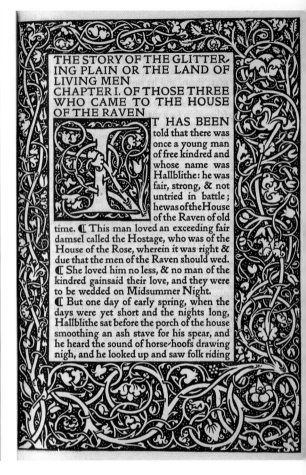

Fig. 22. *Kelmscott Press* [catalog], June 1, 1896. Kelmscott Press, London. Courtesy John M. Kelly Library, St. Michael's College, University of Toronto (via Archive.org)

and 15th-century Venetian models as a foundation, he created the Golden type, named after *The Golden Legend*. Morris would later design Troy, and the smaller Chaucer, both based on the earliest German Gothic models (for examples of the typefaces, see fig. 22). After Edward Prince cut the punches for Golden, the Kelmscott Press began printing. On April 4, 1891, Morris's novel *The Story of the Glittering Plain* became the first book issued by the press (fig. 23).[6]

Fig. 23. *The Story of the Glittering Plain* by William Morris, 1891. Letterpress and wood engraving. The Cleveland Museum of Art, Collection of Ingal Library, Gift of William H. Marlatt and Julia Morgan Marlatt

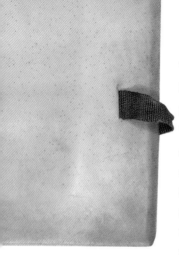

Fig. 24. A typical vellum (parchment)-bound Kelmscott Press book with hand-dyed silk ties (detail of *A Dream of John Ball* and *A King's Lesson*, 1892)

"FOR YOUR TEACHERS, THEY MUST BE NATURE AND HISTORY."[7]

In 1877 Morris proclaimed in his lecture to the Trades' Guild of Learning—later published in *Hopes and Fears for Art* in 1882—that he upheld two models of good design: nature and history. These cornerstones guided his work and determined the appearance of Kelmscott Press publications. By using organic materials, Morris ensured his volumes felt like products of nature, not the mechanized maws of modern industry.[8] The papermaker Joseph Batchelor specially crafted the books' linen rag paper to Morris's specifications. Many of the books are bound in vellum, which Morris preferred to leave plain and unadorned so that its natural variances, including minute hair follicles, gentle ripples, and subtle color modulations, remained perceptible (fig. 24).

Morris's ornaments—initials and borders that he called bloomers and weepers—further link the books to the natural world.[9] His design process is evident in an unfinished border intended, but never used, for a Kelmscott edition of Alfred Tennyson's *Maud* (fig. 25). The designer's hand-drawn scrolling scrim of leaves and vines appears to creep higher and higher toward the light as it materializes. When finished,

Fig. 25. Front-page layout proof for the poem *Maud* by Alfred Tennyson (British, 1809–1892), 1893. William Morris, designer. William Harcourt Hooper, engraver. Kelmscott Press, London. Border with ink and Chinese white, pencil; wood engraving, letterpress; 20.3 x 14.4 cm. Victoria and Albert Museum, London, D.1556-1907. © Victoria and Albert Museum, London

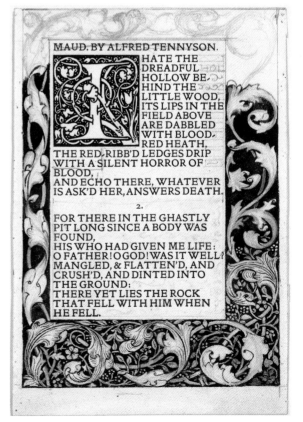

border designs such as these were transferred onto woodblocks, cut by the eminent Victorian wood engraver William Harcourt Hooper, and printed by the Kelmscott pressmen. Although it was a painstaking process, the writer Holbrook Jackson observed that Kelmscott books "convey a sense of inevitability, a feeling that the design is the unconscious blossoming of the page. . . . [They] not only look as if letter and decoration had grown one out of the other; they look as if they could go on growing."[10] Indeed, far from desiccated botanical specimens inside a Victorian book of pressed flowers, the Kelmscott ornaments are perennially vital, weaving together like the timeless words of the texts they surround.

Fig. 26. Frontispiece and title page from *The Work of Geoffrey Chaucer*, 1896. Edward Burne-Jones and William Morris, designers. William Harcourt Hooper, engraver. Letterpress and wood engraving. The Cleveland Museum of Art, Collection of Ingall Library, Gift of William H. Marlatt and Julia Morgan Marlatt

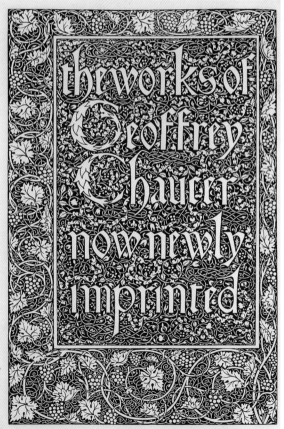

While the foliated borders and initials of a Kelmscott Press book appear as plants growing within an ideal "Earthly Paradise" of Morris's making, the books have engendered other, more colossal comparisons, having been likened to stone architecture rather than organic, living forms. Commenting on the largest Kelmscott book, *The Works of Geoffrey Chaucer*, Burne-Jones remarked that his 87 illustrations, engraved by Hooper to emulate medieval woodcuts, "love[d] to be snugly cased in [Morris's] borders and buttressed up by the vast initials"; he called the volume a "pocket cathedral" (figs. 26, 27).[11] One would be hard-pressed to find a pocket large enough for the 556-page literary monument.

Fig. 27. Illustration for "The Hous of Fame," from *The Works of Geoffrey Chaucer*, 1896. Edward Burne-Jones and William Morris, designers. William Harcourt Hooper, engraver. Letterpress and wood engraving. The Cleveland Museum of Art, Collection of Ingalls Library, Gift of William H. Marlatt and Julia Morgan Marlatt

Aligning the Kelmscott books with Gothic architecture, however, makes sense because Morris's bold ornaments do convey a structural strength: they support Burne-Jones's illuminating illustrations as does carved stone tracery around a stained-glass window.

Burne-Jones and Morris intentionally sought to evoke a Gothic sensibility with their synergetic designs; for inspiration, they pored over Morris's collection of medieval manuscripts and incunabula, or early printed material. Upon completing the illustrations for the second Kelmscott edition of *The Story of the Glittering Plain*, artist Walter Crane wondered if he was "ever quite Gothic enough in feeling to suit [Morris's] taste."[12] Crane's

Fig. 28. Illustration for "They Go from the Isle of Ransom and Come to Cleveland by the Sea," from *The Story of the Glittering Plain* by William Morris, 1894. Walter Crane (British, 1845–1915) and William Morris. Letterpress and wood engraving. The Cleveland Museum of Art, Collection of Ingalls Library, Gift of William H. Marlatt and Julia Morgan Marlatt

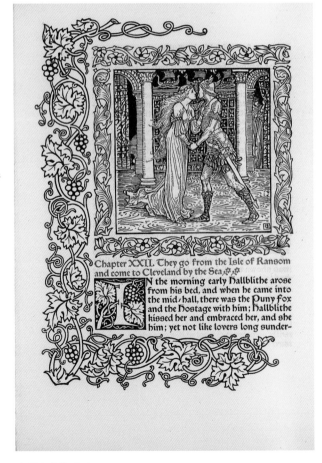

illustration for the chapter "They Go from the Isle of Ransom and Come to Cleveland by the Sea" depicts Hallblithe and the Hostage standing before a colonnade suggestive of a Romanesque cloister (fig. 28). His design for another chapter, "Hallblithe Beholdeth the Woman Who Loveth Him," pictures the Hostage in repose as though she were a sculpted goddess from the pediment of the ancient Greek Parthenon (fig. 29). Similar classical goddess types, seminude figures surrounded by diaphanous drapery, are found in Crane's design for the lusterware "mermaid" vase produced by Maw & Co. in 1889 (fig. 30). Although Burne-Jones also periodically adopted classical models, his lifelong friendship with

Fig. 30. *Lusterware Vase*, 1889. Walter Crane, designer. Maw & Co. (Worcester, est. 1850), manufacturer. Earthenware. Private collection

Chapter XIII. Hallblithe beholdeth the woman who loveth him
UT on the morrow the men arose, & the Sea-eagle and his damsel came to Hallblithe; for the other two damsels were departed, and the

Morris was grounded in a shared love of Chaucer, manuscript illuminations, and woodcuts found in the earliest printed books, thus assuring Morris of the artist's medieval fluency. Indeed, Morris's correspondence with Kelmscott illustrators other than Burne-Jones betrays his anxiety about their specific historical credentials. Dissatisfied with C. M. Gere's illustrations for an unfinished Kelmscott book, *The House of the Wolfings*, Morris advised the young artist to look at "illuminations in 13th & 14th century books." He added, "When I was a young—bear—I think I really succeeded in ignoring modern life altogether. And it was of great service to me."[13]

Fig. 31. *The Nature of Gothic* by John Ruskin (British, 1819–1900), 1892. William Morris. Letterpress and wood engraving. The Cleveland Museum of Art, Collection of Ingalls Library, Gift of William H. Marlatt and Julia Morgan Marlatt

Even Morris's turn to the natural world was part of this historicist impulse, reflective of the romantic Victorian perception that Gothic craftsmen were closer to nature than their 19th-century counterparts. In the title of John Ruskin's influential essay, *The Nature of Gothic*, printed by the Kelmscott Press in 1892, the word *nature* can be read to mean "character," but it also suggests Ruskin's argument that medieval Europe was inherently more "natural" (fig. 31). Ruskin's ode to Gothic architecture and design, first published in 1853 as a chapter in the second volume of *The Stones of Venice*, was interpreted by many in Victorian England as a call to arms against industrialization. It contributed greatly to Morris's own belief in the power of art not only to reflect the society in which it is made but also, when made the right way, to materially and even morally change society for the better. The Kelmscott edition of Ruskin's essay—a collaborative construction from natural materials in a neo-Gothic style—is the ideal vehicle for a message that to Morris "seemed to point out a new road on which the world should travel."[14]

While Kelmscott books evoke the past, they also anticipated such a "new road" for book design in the 1890s. May Morris's father told her, "When you are using an old story, read it through, then shut the book and write it in your own way."[15] This approach to composing poems, novels, and translations helps us understand his general attitude toward design. Never merely bound to the past, Morris's designs looked forward but glanced back for inspiration, mirroring his conception of historical progress. The Kelmscott books exhibit a surprisingly original style, one that was widely copied almost as soon as it appeared. For instance, the Boston publisher Copeland & Day issued several books imitating the Kelmscott aesthetic, including an edition of Dante Gabriel

Fig. 32. *The House of Life* by Dante Gabriel Rossetti (British, 1828–1882), 1894. Bertram Grosvenor Goodhue (American, 1869–1924). Letterpress and wood engraving (?). The Cleveland Museum of Art, Collection of Ingalls Library

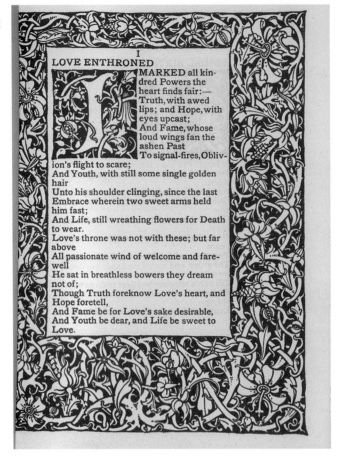

Rossetti's poem *The House of Life*, published in 1894 (fig. 32). Designed by Bertram Grosvenor Goodhue and featuring intricate borders and initials, the book is beautiful in its own right; nonetheless, the pages fail to achieve the palpable vitality of the books so carefully printed by the Kelmscott Press. Goodhue's borders and initials appear static and spiky compared to the fluid acanthus, grapevines, and roses that populate many of Morris's pages.

The prevalence of Kelmscott look-alikes in the 1890s, especially in the United States, speaks to their almost immediate transatlantic popularity. Morris acknowledged this in an 1893 interview with the *Daily Chronicle*, in which he remarked with patent understatement that he had "a small public in America."[16] Individual American collectors and booksellers appear with some frequency in the Kelmscott Press mailing list. During the 1890s, book lovers in Cleveland could purchase volumes from the downtown bookseller Burrows Brothers. In Chicago, the publisher Way and Williams approached the press in 1895 to print an edition of Rossetti's *Hand and Soul*; 200 copies of it were produced especially for American distribution. The second-hand market, which emerged as soon as the books left the press, was particularly robust in the United States. At the turn of the century, auctions of the books in New York City garnered record prices, and American collectors in the first decades of the 20th century frequently purchased them from sellers and auction houses in the United Kingdom.

It is within this milieu that Clevelanders William and Julia Marlatt amassed a complete set of Kelmscott Press books, a collection that would eventually form part of their generous bequest to the Cleveland Museum of Art. There is scant documentation relating to the Marlatts' collection, although there exists a receipt for volume 1 of *The Golden Legend*, purchased from the London bookseller Bernard Quaritch Ltd. in 1917. The Marlatts' edition of Sir Thomas More's *Utopia* was probably purchased at auction from Sotheby's in 1919. A unique presentation copy, it was originally given to the Victorian literary scholar F. J. Furnivall by the Kelmscott Press's editor F. S. Ellis. As Louis Adrean and Marsha Morrow reveal in their article "A Quiet Bequest," the gift of the books, along with other important works of art and a substantial amount of money, came as a surprise to the museum.[17] The Marlatts discreetly amassed and enjoyed their collection, with few people aware of its existence. Although the beautiful volumes printed by the Kelmscott Press quickly became valuable collectors' items, William Morris chose to believe that the majority of them were "bought, not so much by folks who desire to say they have them, as by those who really wish to have them for their own sake."[18] Although we cannot know for sure, it is perhaps in this spirit that the Marlatts quietly cherished their Kelmscott books, not merely as precious commodities but as beautiful works of art—glimmers of Morris's idea of an "Earthly Paradise" on its way to being achieved.

Victoria Hepburn is currently pursuing a PhD from Yale University's Department of the History of Art, with a focus on 19th-century Britain.

1. William Morris, "The Ideal Book" (1893), in *The Ideal Book: Essays and Lectures on the Arts of the Book*, ed. William S. Peterson (Berkeley: University of California, 1982), 73.

2. "'Master Printer Morris': A Visit to the Kelmscott Press," *Daily Chronicle*, February 22, 1893; reprinted in Morris, *The Ideal Book*, 95.

3. Paul Needham, "William Morris: Book Collector," in *William Morris and the Art of the Book*, by Paul Needham, Joseph Dunlap, and John Dreyfus (London: Oxford University Press, 1976), 29.

4. See Joseph R. Dunlap, *The Book That Never Was* (New York: Oriole, 1971), 28.

5. William Morris, letter to Frederick Startridge Ellis, November 21, 1889, in *The Collected Letters of William Morris*, ed. Norman Kelvin (Princeton, NJ: Princeton University Press, 2014), 3:124. Morris wrote: "I really am thinking of turning printer myself in a small way; the first step to that would be getting a new fount cut."

6. For more on the founding of the Kelmscott Press, see William S. Peterson, *The Kelmscott Press: A History of William Morris's Typographical Adventure* (New York: Oxford University Press, 1991).

7. William Morris, "Hopes and Fears for Art," in *The Collected Works of William Morris: With Introductions by His Daughter May Morris*, vol. 22 (Cambridge: Cambridge University Press, 2012), 15.

8. See Nicholas Frankel, "The Ecology of Decoration: Design and Environment in the Writings of William Morris," *Journal of Pre-Raphaelite Studies* 12 (Fall 2003): 78–81.

9. "'Master Printer Morris,'" 95.

10. Holbrook Jackson, *The Eighteen Nineties: A Review of Art and Ideas at the Close of the Nineteenth Century* (London: Grant Richards, 1922), 263.

11. Peterson, *Kelmscott Press*, 164.

12. Peterson, 156.

13. William Morris, letter to Charles March Gere, November 7, 1893, in Kelvin, *Collected Letters*, 4:101.

14. William Morris, preface to *The Nature of Gothic*, by John Ruskin and William Morris (London: Kelmscott Press, 1892), i.

15. May Morris, introduction to *The Collected Works of William Morris: With Introductions by His Daughter May Morris*, vol. 3 (London: Longmans, Green, 1910–15), xxii.

16. "'Master Printer Morris,'" 95.

17. Louis V. Adrean and Marsha A. Morrow, "A Quiet Bequest," *Cleveland Art: The Cleveland Museum of Art Members Magazine*, September 2006, 13.

18. "'Master Printer Morris,'" 95.

Further Readings

Faulkner, Peter. *Against the Age: An Introduction to William Morris*. London: Allen & Unwin, 1980.

Harvey, Charles, and Jon Press. *William Morris: Design and Enterprise in Victorian Britain*. Manchester: Manchester University Press, 1991.

Kelvin, Norman, ed. *The Collected Letters of William Morris: 1848–1896*. 3 vols. Princeton, NJ: Princeton University Press, 1984–96.

Lister, Jenny, Jan Marsh, and Anna Mason, eds. *May Morris: Arts & Crafts Designer*. London: Thames & Hudson, 2017.

MacCarthy, Fiona. *William Morris: A Life for Our Time*. London: Faber & Faber, 1994.

Mackail, John W. *The Life of William Morris*. 2 vols. London: Longmans, Green, 1899.

Marsh, Jan. *Jane and May Morris: A Biographical Story, 1839–1938*. London: Pandora, 1986.

———. *William Morris and Red House*. London: National Trust Books, 2005.

Miele, Chris, ed. *From William Morris: Building Conservation and the Arts and Crafts Cult of Authenticity, 1877–1939*. New Haven, CT: Yale University Press, 2005.

Morris, May, ed. *The Collected Works of William Morris*. 24 vols. London: Longmans, Green, 1910–15.

———. *William Morris: Artist, Writer, Socialist*. 2 vols. Oxford: Basil Blackwell, 1936.

Needham, Paul, Joseph Dunlap, and John Dreyfus. *William Morris and the Art of the Book*. London: Oxford University Press, 1976.

Parry, Linda. *William Morris*. Exh. cat. London: Philip Wilson; Victoria and Albert Museum, 1996.

———. *William Morris Textiles*. London: V&A Publishing, 2013.

Peterson, William S., ed. *The Ideal Book: Essays and Lectures on the Arts of the Book*. Berkeley: University of California, 1982.

———. *The Kelmscott Press: A History of William Morris's Typographical Adventure*. New York: Oxford University Press, 1991.

Thompson, Paul. *The Work of William Morris*. New York: Viking, 1967.

Todd, Pamela. *William Morris and the Arts and Crafts Home*. San Francisco: Chronicle Books, 2005.

Vallance, Aymer. *William Morris: His Art, His Writings and His Public Life*. London: George Bell & Sons, 1898.

Watkinson, Raymond. *William Morris as Designer*. London: Studio Vista, 1967.

Whipple, David. "Textile Designs and Books by William Morris." *Bulletin of the Cleveland Museum of Art* 65, no. 7 (1978): 247–57.

Wilmer, Clive, ed. *William Morris: "News from Nowhere" and Other Writings*. London: Penguin Classics, 1993.